ADHD
Introduction to a Neurodiverse World

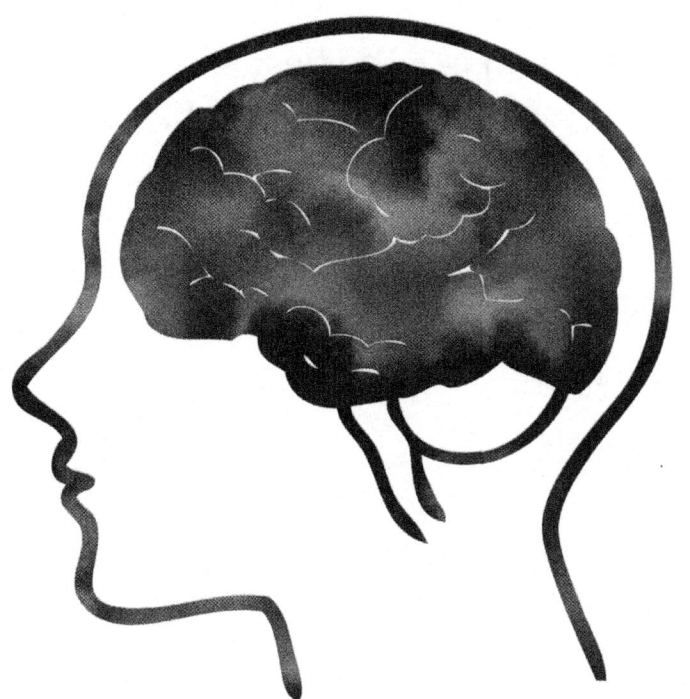

Gareth Croot
Published by Divergent Consultants

Foreword

I was going to publish this book on 10th March 2023 but I Procrastinated and got side tracked.

And if that isn't the best start to this book, I don't know what is!

Contents

1. What is ADHD? A Brief Overview of the Disorder
2. The Neurodiversity Movement and the Importance of Understanding ADHD
3. Understanding ADHD from a Developmental Perspective
4. The Different Types of ADHD and Their Characteristics
5. The Genetics of ADHD: Is it in the DNA?
6. The Environmental Factors that Contribute to ADHD
7. The Relationship between ADHD and Executive Functioning
8. The Emotional Impacts of ADHD
9. ADHD and Academic Success: Challenges and Strategies
10. The Connection Between ADHD and Creativity
11. The Connection between ADHD and Entrepreneurship
12. The Connection Between ADHD and Innovation
13. ADHD and Relationships: Navigating Social Interactions
14. The Connection Between ADHD and Substance Abuse
15. The Connection Between ADHD and Sleep Disorders
16. The Connection Between ADHD and Anxiety Disorders
17. The Connection Between ADHD and Depression
18. ADHD and Employment: Challenges and Strategies
19. ADHD and Parenting: Navigating the Challenges
20. ADHD and Advocacy: Empowering Neurodiverse Individuals

What is ADHD? A Brief Overview of the Disorder

Attention Deficit Hyperactivity Disorder, commonly known as ADHD, is a neurodevelopmental disorder that affects millions of people worldwide. ADHD is typically diagnosed in childhood, although it can persist into adulthood. This disorder can significantly impact a person's daily life and often requires ongoing management and treatment.

The defining features of ADHD are inattention, hyperactivity, and impulsivity. However, not all individuals with ADHD exhibit all three of these features. The severity of these symptoms can also vary greatly between individuals. In some cases, the symptoms of ADHD may be so severe that they significantly impact the individual's academic, social, and occupational functioning.

There are three subtypes of ADHD: predominantly inattentive type, predominantly hyperactive-impulsive type, and combined type. The predominantly inattentive type is characterized by symptoms of inattention, such as difficulty paying attention, being forgetful, and having trouble following through on instructions. The predominantly hyperactive-impulsive type is characterized by symptoms of hyperactivity and impulsivity, such as excessive fidgeting, difficulty sitting still, and interrupting others. The combined type is the most common subtype and includes symptoms of both inattention and hyperactivity/impulsivity.

The cause of ADHD is not fully understood. However, research has suggested that genetics play a significant role in the development of the disorder. Studies have also shown that environmental factors, such as prenatal exposure to nicotine and alcohol, may increase the risk of developing ADHD. Additionally, there may be other factors at play, such as alterations in brain structure and function.

ADHD is a diagnosis that can only be made by a qualified medical professional, such as a psychiatrist, psychologist, or pediatrician. The diagnosis process typically involves a comprehensive evaluation of the individual's medical history, symptoms, and behavior. In some cases, other medical conditions may need to be ruled out before a diagnosis of ADHD can be made.

Once an individual has been diagnosed with ADHD, a treatment plan will be developed. The most common treatment options for ADHD include medication, therapy, or a combination of the two. Medications, such as stimulants and non-stimulants, are often used to manage the symptoms of ADHD. Therapy may include behavioral therapy, cognitive-behavioral therapy, or social skills training. Additionally, lifestyle changes, such as regular exercise, a healthy diet, and good sleep hygiene, may also be recommended.

It is important to note that ADHD is not a result of poor parenting, lack of discipline, or a lack of intelligence. ADHD is a neurodevelopmental disorder that affects the way the brain functions. Individuals with ADHD often have difficulty with executive functioning, which includes skills such as organization, time management, and prioritization. As a result, individuals with ADHD may struggle with tasks that require these skills.

The impact of ADHD on an individual's daily life can be significant. In children, ADHD can impact academic performance, social relationships, and behavior. Adults with ADHD may struggle with maintaining employment, managing finances, and maintaining personal relationships. The stigma associated with ADHD can also be a significant barrier to treatment and support.

In the United Kingdom, the National Institute for Health and Care Excellence (NICE) provides guidelines for the assessment and management of ADHD. These guidelines recommend that an initial assessment be conducted by a specialist, such as a pediatrician or psychiatrist. The guidelines also recommend that medication be considered as a first-line treatment option for individuals with moderate to severe ADHD. Additionally, the guidelines recommend that support be provided for the individual and their family, including education about the disorder, social skills training, and assistance with school or work accommodations.

Despite the challenges associated with ADHD, many individuals with the disorder have gone on to achieve great success in a variety of fields. Famous individuals with ADHD include Michael Phelps, Simone Biles, and Justin Timberlake. It is important to recognize that individuals with ADHD have unique strengths and abilities that can be harnessed with the right support and management strategies.

One of the most important aspects of managing ADHD is developing a support system. This may include working closely with a medical professional, seeking out therapy, and building a support network of family and friends. In addition, individuals with ADHD may benefit from education about the disorder and strategies for managing their symptoms. This can include learning about time management techniques, organization strategies, and stress reduction techniques.

It is also important to recognize the impact of ADHD on the family and loved ones of individuals with the disorder. Parents of children with ADHD may experience significant stress and frustration in managing their child's behavior and symptoms. Partners of adults with ADHD may struggle with communication and understanding their partner's challenges. Family therapy and support groups can be helpful resources for addressing these challenges.

In recent years, there has been a growing recognition of the importance of neurodiversity and the value of individuals with ADHD and other neurodevelopmental disorders. Neurodiversity refers to the concept that neurological differences are a natural variation in human diversity, rather than a disorder or deficit. By embracing neurodiversity, we can work to create a more inclusive and accepting society that values individuals for their unique strengths and abilities.

The Neurodiversity Movement and the Importance of Understanding ADHD

The concept of neurodiversity has been gaining momentum in recent years, and with it, a growing recognition of the importance of understanding ADHD and other neurodevelopmental disorders. The neurodiversity movement is centered around the belief that neurological differences are a natural variation in human diversity, rather than a disorder or deficit. By embracing neurodiversity, we can work to create a more inclusive and accepting society that values individuals for their unique strengths and abilities.

ADHD, or Attention-Deficit/Hyperactivity Disorder, is a neurodevelopmental disorder that affects millions of people worldwide. The disorder is characterized by inattention, hyperactivity, and impulsivity, and can significantly impact an individual's daily life. While the cause of ADHD is not fully understood, research has suggested that genetics and environmental factors may play a role.

The neurodiversity movement challenges the traditional medical model of viewing ADHD as a disorder that needs to be fixed or cured. Instead, it recognizes the value of individuals with ADHD and other neurodevelopmental differences, and works to promote acceptance and accommodation for their unique needs.

One of the key tenets of the neurodiversity movement is the idea of universal design. Universal design is the concept of designing products, services, and environments that are accessible and usable by everyone, regardless of their abilities or disabilities. This can include things like ergonomic furniture, assistive technology, and sensory-friendly environments.

For individuals with ADHD, universal design can be particularly important. For example, creating a quiet workspace with minimal distractions can be helpful for individuals with ADHD who struggle with inattention. Providing clear instructions and breaking tasks down into manageable steps can also be helpful for individuals with ADHD who struggle with executive function.

In addition to universal design, the neurodiversity movement emphasizes the importance of accommodations and support for individuals with ADHD. This can include things like extended time on tests, preferential seating in the classroom, and access to assistive technology. By providing these accommodations and supports, individuals with ADHD can be more successful in school, work, and other areas of life.

Another important aspect of the neurodiversity movement is the recognition of the impact of ADHD on mental health. Individuals with ADHD are at a higher risk of developing anxiety, depression, and other mental health conditions. It is important to provide support and resources for addressing these challenges, including therapy, medication, and mindfulness practices.

The neurodiversity movement also challenges stereotypes and stigmas associated with ADHD and other neurodevelopmental differences. For example, individuals with ADHD are often viewed as lazy or unmotivated, when in reality, they may be struggling with executive function and other symptoms of the disorder. By recognizing the unique strengths and abilities of individuals with ADHD, we can challenge these stereotypes and promote a more positive and accepting view of neurodiversity.

In recent years, there has been a growing recognition of the importance of understanding and accommodating ADHD in the workplace. Many employers are implementing policies and practices to support neurodiverse employees, including flexible schedules, accommodations for sensory sensitivities, and training for managers on working with individuals with ADHD. By creating a more inclusive and accommodating workplace, employers can benefit from the unique strengths and abilities of individuals with ADHD.

Finally, it is important to recognize the role of advocacy and activism in the neurodiversity movement. By speaking out about their experiences and advocating for their needs, individuals with ADHD and other neurodiverse conditions can create change and promote acceptance in society. This can include participating in research studies, advocating for policy changes, and educating others about the importance of neurodiversity.

Understanding ADHD from a Developmental Perspective

Understanding ADHD from a developmental perspective can provide valuable insights into the disorder and how it affects individuals across the lifespan. Developmental psychology is the study of how people change and grow over time, from infancy through adulthood.

In the case of ADHD, developmental psychology can help us understand how the disorder impacts individuals at different stages of development. For example, research has shown that ADHD symptoms can manifest differently in children, adolescents, and adults. By understanding these developmental differences, we can provide more targeted interventions and support for individuals with ADHD.

In children, ADHD is often characterized by hyperactivity and impulsivity, along with inattention. Children with ADHD may struggle with following directions, completing tasks, and paying attention in school. They may also have difficulty with social interactions and regulating their emotions.

It is important to note that some degree of hyperactivity and impulsivity is typical in young children, and not all children who are active or impulsive have ADHD. However, when these behaviours are significantly more frequent or intense than what is typical for a child's age and developmental level, ADHD may be a possibility.

In adolescence, ADHD symptoms may become more focused on inattention and difficulties with executive function, such as planning and organization. Adolescents with ADHD may struggle with academic tasks, particularly those that require sustained attention and effort. They may also have difficulty with social skills, such as making and maintaining friendships.

In adulthood, ADHD symptoms may continue to impact daily life, particularly in areas such as employment and relationships. Adults with ADHD may struggle with time management, organization, and completing tasks. They may also experience challenges with maintaining relationships, particularly in terms of communication and emotional regulation.

One important aspect of understanding ADHD from a developmental perspective is recognizing that the disorder can impact individuals differently based on their gender. While ADHD is diagnosed more frequently in males than females, research suggests that females may be underdiagnosed or misdiagnosed due to differences in how symptoms present.

For example, females with ADHD may be more likely to exhibit symptoms of inattention and anxiety, rather than hyperactivity and impulsivity. They may also be better at masking their symptoms in social situations, which can make it more difficult to recognize the disorder.

Understanding the impact of ADHD on development can also help us understand the potential long-term consequences of the disorder. For example, research has shown that individuals with ADHD are at higher risk for academic underachievement, social difficulties, and mental health problems.

However, it is important to note that not all individuals with ADHD will experience negative outcomes, and many individuals with the disorder are able to live successful and fulfilling lives with appropriate support and interventions.

Treatment for ADHD typically includes a combination of medication, therapy, and behavioral interventions. Medication can help reduce symptoms of inattention and hyperactivity, while therapy can provide support and strategies for managing the challenges of the disorder. Behavioural interventions, such as parent training and classroom accommodations, can also be helpful in managing ADHD symptoms.

The Different Types of ADHD and Their Characteristics

There are three different types of ADHD, each with its own set of characteristics. Understanding the different types of ADHD can help individuals with the disorder receive more targeted interventions and support.

The three types of ADHD are:

Predominantly Inattentive Type

This type of ADHD is characterized by significant difficulties with attention and focus, but less hyperactivity and impulsivity. Individuals with predominantly inattentive ADHD may struggle with paying attention in school or work, following instructions, and completing tasks. They may appear forgetful, disorganized, and easily distracted. They may also struggle with executive function, such as planning and organizing.

Predominantly Hyperactive-Impulsive Type

This type of ADHD is characterized by significant hyperactivity and impulsivity, but less difficulty with attention and focus. Individuals with predominantly hyperactive-impulsive ADHD may struggle with sitting still, fidgeting, and interrupting others. They may also have difficulty waiting their turn, taking turns, and following rules. They may be prone to accidents and injuries due to their impulsivity and lack of caution.

Combined Type

This type of ADHD is characterized by significant difficulties with both attention and hyperactivity/impulsivity. Individuals with combined type ADHD may struggle with all of the symptoms of inattention and hyperactivity/impulsivity. They may have difficulty sitting still, staying focused on tasks, and controlling their impulses. This is the most common type of ADHD.

It is important to note that the symptoms of ADHD can vary widely between individuals, even within the same type of ADHD. For example, one individual with predominantly inattentive ADHD may struggle primarily with forgetfulness and disorganization, while another may struggle primarily with distractibility and difficulty following instructions.

Additionally, the severity of ADHD symptoms can vary widely between individuals, even within the same type of ADHD. Some individuals may have mild symptoms that do not significantly impact their daily life, while others may have severe symptoms that significantly impact their daily life.

Understanding the different types of ADHD can be helpful in providing targeted interventions and support for individuals with the disorder. For example, individuals with predominantly inattentive ADHD may benefit from strategies to improve attention and executive function, such as mindfulness techniques and organizational tools. Individuals with predominantly hyperactive-impulsive ADHD may benefit from strategies to improve impulse control and emotional regulation, such as cognitive-behavioral therapy and stress management techniques.

Treatment for ADHD typically includes a combination of medication, therapy, and behavioral interventions. Medication can help reduce symptoms of inattention and hyperactivity, while therapy can provide support and strategies for managing the challenges of the disorder. Behavioural interventions, such as parent training and classroom accommodations, can also be helpful in managing ADHD symptoms.

It is important to note that the different types of ADHD are not mutually exclusive, and individuals with ADHD may exhibit symptoms from multiple types. For example, an individual with predominantly inattentive ADHD may also exhibit some hyperactivity and impulsivity. It is also possible for the type of ADHD to change over time, particularly as individuals move through different stages of development.

In addition to the different types of ADHD, there are also other subtypes of ADHD that can impact individuals in different ways. For example, research has suggested that some individuals with ADHD may exhibit symptoms primarily in specific situations, such as during academic tasks or social interactions. These subtypes of ADHD may require different interventions and support than the traditional types of ADHD.

The Genetics of ADHD: Is it in the DNA?

Attention-Deficit/Hyperactivity Disorder (ADHD) is a neurodevelopmental disorder that affects millions of people worldwide. While the exact causes of ADHD are still not fully understood, research has suggested that genetics may play a significant role in the development of the disorder. In this chapter, we will explore the genetics of ADHD and what current research has to say about the role of DNA in the development of ADHD.

What is ADHD?

Before we dive into the genetics of ADHD, it is important to understand what the disorder is and how it impacts individuals. ADHD is characterized by inattention, hyperactivity, and impulsivity, and can significantly impact an individual's daily life. Symptoms of ADHD can include difficulty paying attention, forgetting things, being easily distracted, fidgeting, restlessness, talking excessively, interrupting others, and difficulty waiting their turn.

ADHD is typically diagnosed in childhood but can also be diagnosed in adulthood. The disorder is often chronic and can persist into adulthood, although symptoms may change over time. Treatment for ADHD typically includes a combination of medication, therapy, and behavioral interventions.

The Role of Genetics in ADHD

While the exact causes of ADHD are still not fully understood, research has suggested that genetics may play a significant role in the development of the disorder. Studies of families with ADHD have found that the disorder tends to run in families, with individuals who have a close relative with ADHD being more likely to develop the disorder themselves.

Research has also identified specific genes that may be associated with an increased risk of developing ADHD. For example, studies have suggested that variations in the genes that regulate dopamine, a neurotransmitter that plays a key role in reward and motivation, may be associated with an increased risk of developing ADHD. Other genes that have been implicated in the development of ADHD include those involved in the regulation of serotonin, a neurotransmitter that plays a role in mood regulation and impulse control, and those involved in the development of the brain's prefrontal cortex, which is responsible for executive function.

It is important to note that while genetics may play a significant role in the development of ADHD, it is not the only factor involved. Environmental factors, such as prenatal exposure to toxins and maternal smoking during pregnancy, have also been associated with an increased risk of developing ADHD.

The Importance of Understanding the Genetics of ADHD

Understanding the genetics of ADHD can be helpful in several ways. First, it can help individuals with ADHD and their families understand that the disorder is not their fault, and that there are biological factors involved in its development. This can help reduce feelings of guilt and shame that individuals with ADHD may experience.

Second, understanding the genetics of ADHD can help healthcare professionals provide more targeted interventions and support for individuals with the disorder. For example, genetic testing may be able to identify specific genes that are associated with an increased risk of developing ADHD, which can help inform treatment decisions.

Third, understanding the genetics of ADHD can help researchers develop new treatments for the disorder. By identifying specific genes and pathways that are involved in the development of ADHD, researchers may be able to develop more targeted and effective treatments for the disorder.

Limitations of Research on the Genetics of ADHD

While research on the genetics of ADHD has provided valuable insights into the development of the disorder, there are also limitations to this research. One limitation is that ADHD is a complex disorder with multiple genetic and environmental factors involved, making it difficult to pinpoint specific genes that are responsible for the development of the disorder.

Another limitation is that genetic testing for ADHD is not yet widely available or clinically validated. While some genetic tests for ADHD are currently available, their accuracy and clinical utility are still being evaluated. Additionally, genetic testing for ADHD is not currently recommended as a routine part of ADHD diagnosis or treatment.

The Environmental Factors that Contribute to ADHD

Environmental Factors that Contribute to ADHD

Prenatal Exposure to Toxins: Exposure to environmental toxins, such as lead and pesticides, during pregnancy has been linked to an increased risk of developing ADHD. These toxins can cross the placenta and enter the developing foetus, disrupting brain development and potentially increasing the risk of ADHD.

Maternal Smoking During Pregnancy: Studies have shown that maternal smoking during pregnancy is associated with an increased risk of ADHD in children. Nicotine and other chemicals in cigarettes can cross the placenta and enter the developing foetus, potentially disrupting brain development and increasing the risk of ADHD.

Premature Birth: Premature birth has been linked to an increased risk of ADHD. This may be because premature infants are more vulnerable to brain injury and abnormal brain development.

Low Birth Weight: Low birth weight has also been linked to an increased risk of ADHD. This may be because low birth weight infants are more vulnerable to brain injury and abnormal brain development.

Early Childhood Adversity: Adverse experiences in early childhood, such as neglect or abuse, have been linked to an increased risk of ADHD. These experiences can cause chronic stress and disrupt brain development, potentially increasing the risk of ADHD.

Sleep Problems: Sleep problems, such as sleep apnea or restless leg syndrome, have been linked to an increased risk of ADHD. This may be because disrupted sleep can affect brain development and function.

Reducing the Impact of Environmental Factors on ADHD

While it may not be possible to completely eliminate the impact of environmental factors on ADHD, there are steps that can be taken to reduce their impact.

Avoid Exposure to Toxins: Pregnant women and young children should avoid exposure to environmental toxins, such as lead and pesticides, as much as possible. This may involve making changes to the home environment, such as using non-toxic cleaning products and avoiding the use of pesticides.

Quit Smoking: Pregnant women should quit smoking to reduce the risk of ADHD in their children. If you are struggling to quit smoking, talk to your healthcare provider about resources that can help.

Seek Early Intervention for Premature and Low Birth Weight Infants: Premature and low birth weight infants may benefit from early intervention services, such as developmental therapy or speech therapy, to support their development.

Provide a Stable and Nurturing Environment: Children who have experienced early childhood adversity may benefit from a stable and nurturing environment that promotes their social, emotional, and cognitive development. This may involve seeking support from a therapist or social worker, and connecting with community resources that can help.

Address Sleep Problems: Children who have sleep problems should be evaluated by a healthcare provider to identify and treat any underlying conditions that may be contributing to their sleep difficulties.

It is important to note that not all individuals with ADHD have experienced these environmental factors, and not all individuals who have experienced these factors will develop ADHD. ADHD is a complex disorder that is influenced by a variety of factors, and research is ongoing to better understand its causes and develop effective treatments.

If you or a loved one are concerned about ADHD or are experiencing symptoms of the disorder, it is important to seek guidance from a healthcare professional. A healthcare provider can help evaluate symptoms, provide a diagnosis, and develop a treatment plan tailored to the individual's needs.

The Relationship between ADHD and Executive Functioning

Attention Deficit Hyperactivity Disorder (ADHD) is a neurodevelopmental disorder that affects millions of people worldwide. One of the most significant challenges associated with ADHD is the impact on executive functioning, which can have significant consequences for individuals in many areas of their lives. In this chapter, we will explore the relationship between ADHD and executive functioning and discuss some strategies for managing symptoms.

What is Executive Functioning?

Executive functioning refers to the cognitive processes that enable individuals to plan, organize, problem-solve, initiate tasks, and regulate their behavior. It is a set of mental skills that helps us manage our lives and navigate complex situations. Executive functioning includes several interrelated abilities, including working memory, cognitive flexibility, inhibition, and self-control.

Working memory is the ability to hold information in mind and manipulate it. Cognitive flexibility is the ability to switch between tasks and adapt to new situations. Inhibition is the ability to control impulses and regulate behavior. Self-control refers to the ability to regulate emotions and manage distractions.

Executive functioning is critical for academic success, social relationships, and daily life. Individuals with ADHD often experience challenges in these areas due to difficulties with executive functioning.

The Relationship between ADHD and Executive Functioning

ADHD is characterized by difficulties with attention, hyperactivity, and impulsivity. These symptoms are often associated with deficits in executive functioning. Individuals with ADHD often struggle with tasks that require working memory, cognitive flexibility, inhibition, and self-control. For example, a child with ADHD may have difficulty completing homework assignments or staying focused during class due to poor working memory. An adult with ADHD may struggle with organization and time management due to poor inhibition and self-control.

Research has shown that individuals with ADHD have structural and functional differences in the areas of the brain that are involved in executive functioning. These differences can affect the neural pathways that support these abilities, leading to difficulties in planning, organizing, and regulating behavior.

Managing ADHD and Executive Functioning

Fortunately, there are several strategies that individuals with ADHD can use to manage their symptoms and improve executive functioning. These strategies include:

Medication: Medication is a common treatment for ADHD that can help improve executive functioning by increasing the availability of neurotransmitters in the brain.

Cognitive-behavioral therapy (CBT): CBT is a form of therapy that helps individuals identify negative thought patterns and develop more adaptive coping strategies. CBT can be particularly effective for improving executive functioning by helping individuals learn to regulate their behavior and manage distractions.

Mindfulness: Mindfulness is a practice that involves focusing on the present moment without judgment. It can help individuals with ADHD develop better self-awareness, reduce stress, and improve working memory.

Exercise: Exercise is a natural mood-booster that can help improve executive functioning by increasing blood flow to the brain and promoting the growth of new neural connections.

Sleep: Adequate sleep is essential for maintaining executive functioning. Individuals with ADHD should aim to get 7-9 hours of sleep per night and develop a consistent sleep routine.

The Emotional Impacts of ADHD

Attention Deficit Hyperactivity Disorder (ADHD) is a neurodevelopmental disorder that affects millions of people worldwide. While many people are familiar with the classic symptoms of ADHD, such as hyperactivity, impulsivity, and difficulty with attention, less is known about the emotional impacts of the disorder. In this chapter, we will explore the emotional impacts of ADHD and discuss strategies for managing them.

The Emotional Impacts of ADHD

ADHD can have significant emotional impacts on individuals of all ages. Some of the most common emotional impacts of ADHD include:

Frustration and irritability: Individuals with ADHD often struggle with impulse control and may become easily frustrated or irritated.

Anxiety and worry: Difficulty with attention and organization can lead to feelings of anxiety and worry, particularly in academic or work settings.

Low self-esteem: The challenges associated with ADHD can lead to feelings of inadequacy and low self-esteem.

Depression: Individuals with ADHD are at an increased risk of developing depression, particularly in adolescence and adulthood.

Difficulty with emotional regulation: Individuals with ADHD may struggle to regulate their emotions, leading to outbursts or inappropriate emotional responses.

Managing the Emotional Impacts of ADHD

Fortunately, there are several strategies that individuals with ADHD can use to manage the emotional impacts of the disorder. These strategies include:

Medication: Medication is a common treatment for ADHD that can help improve emotional regulation by increasing the availability of neurotransmitters in the brain.

Cognitive-behavioral therapy (CBT): CBT is a form of therapy that can help individuals identify negative thought patterns and develop more adaptive coping strategies. CBT can be particularly effective for managing the emotional impacts of ADHD by helping individuals develop strategies for regulating their emotions and managing stress.

Mindfulness: Mindfulness is a practice that involves focusing on the present moment without judgment. It can help individuals with ADHD develop better self-awareness, reduce stress, and regulate their emotions.

Exercise: Exercise is a natural mood-booster that can help improve emotional regulation by increasing blood flow to the brain and promoting the release of endorphins.

Social support: Building a support network of friends, family, and healthcare professionals can help individuals with ADHD feel less isolated and better equipped to manage their emotions.

ADHD and Academic Success: Challenges and Strategies

Attention Deficit Hyperactivity Disorder (ADHD) is a neurodevelopmental disorder that can affect academic performance in many ways. Individuals with ADHD may struggle with attention, organization, planning, and time management, all of which can impact academic success. However, with the right strategies and support, individuals with ADHD can achieve academic success. In this chapter, we will explore the challenges faced by individuals with ADHD in academic settings and discuss strategies for success.

Challenges Faced by Individuals with ADHD in Academic Settings

Attention and Focus: Individuals with ADHD may struggle with paying attention in class or while studying, leading to missed information and difficulty retaining information.

Organization and Planning: Individuals with ADHD may struggle with organizing materials, planning assignments, and breaking down larger projects into manageable tasks.

Time Management: Individuals with ADHD may struggle with managing time effectively, leading to procrastination and missed deadlines.

Impulsivity: Individuals with ADHD may struggle with impulse control, leading to distracted behavior or speaking out of turn in class.

Memory: Individuals with ADHD may struggle with short-term memory, leading to difficulty remembering information for exams or tests.

Strategies for Academic Success for Individuals with ADHD

Create a Structured Study Environment: Creating a structured study environment with minimal distractions can help individuals with ADHD focus and retain information more effectively. Consider studying in a quiet library or a designated study space at home.

Use a Planner or Calendar: Using a planner or calendar can help individuals with ADHD keep track of assignments and deadlines, as well as prioritize tasks.

Break Down Assignments: Breaking down larger assignments into smaller, manageable tasks can help individuals with ADHD stay organized and avoid feeling overwhelmed.

Use Visual Aids: Using visual aids such as charts or diagrams can help individuals with ADHD better understand and retain information.

Seek Accommodations: Individuals with ADHD may be eligible for academic accommodations such as extended time on exams or note-taking assistance. Speak with a school counsellor or disabilities office to explore available options.

Take Breaks: Taking frequent breaks while studying or completing assignments can help individuals with ADHD maintain focus and avoid burnout.

Stay Active: Engaging in physical activity such as exercise or sports can help individuals with ADHD manage symptoms such as impulsivity and hyperactivity, leading to improved academic performance.

Utilize Technology: Technology such as computer programs or apps can help individuals with ADHD stay organized, manage time, and improve focus.

ADHD can present significant challenges in academic settings, but with the right strategies and support, individuals with ADHD can achieve academic success. Strategies such as creating a structured study environment, using a planner or calendar, and breaking down assignments can help individuals with ADHD stay organized and manage their time effectively. Seeking accommodations, taking frequent breaks, staying active, and utilizing technology can also help individuals with ADHD manage symptoms and improve academic performance. It is important for individuals with ADHD to seek guidance and support from healthcare professionals, school counsellors, and other resources to help manage the challenges associated with ADHD. By adopting effective strategies and seeking support, individuals with ADHD can thrive academically and achieve their goals.

The Connection Between ADHD and Creativity

Attention Deficit Hyperactivity Disorder (ADHD) is a neurodevelopmental disorder that affects attention, focus, and impulse control. However, research has shown that there may be a link between ADHD and creativity. In this chapter, we will explore the connection between ADHD and creativity and how individuals with ADHD can harness their creativity to their advantage.

ADHD and Creativity

Studies have found that individuals with ADHD are more likely to engage in creative activities and pursue creative careers. For example, a study published in the Journal of Creative Behaviour found that individuals with ADHD were more likely to have creative achievements, such as writing, art, and music, than those without ADHD. Additionally, a study published in the Journal of Abnormal Psychology found that individuals with ADHD were more likely to have a creative thinking style, which is characterized by unconventional thinking and problem-solving.

One theory for why there may be a connection between ADHD and creativity is that individuals with ADHD have a different way of processing information. The brains of individuals with ADHD may be wired differently, allowing for more fluid and unconventional thinking. This can lead to creative ideas and solutions that may not have been considered by individuals without ADHD.

Harnessing Creativity for Individuals with ADHD

While creativity can be a strength for individuals with ADHD, it can also pose challenges. Individuals with ADHD may struggle with organization and follow-through, which can impede the creative process. Additionally, individuals with ADHD may struggle with distractions, leading to difficulty staying on task and completing creative projects.

Here are some strategies for harnessing creativity for individuals with ADHD:

Set Boundaries: While it is important to allow time for creative pursuits, it is also important to set boundaries and structure. Setting aside designated time for creative projects and creating a schedule can help individuals with ADHD stay on task and avoid distraction.

Break Projects into Smaller Tasks: Breaking larger creative projects into smaller, manageable tasks can help individuals with ADHD stay organized and avoid feeling overwhelmed.

Use a Creative Outlet to Manage ADHD Symptoms: Engaging in creative activities such as drawing, painting, or writing can help individuals with ADHD manage symptoms such as impulsivity and hyperactivity.

Use Visual Aids: Using visual aids such as charts or diagrams can help individuals with ADHD better understand and retain information, leading to improved creative output.

Collaborate: Collaborating with others on creative projects can help individuals with ADHD stay on task and avoid procrastination. Additionally, working with others can provide different perspectives and inspire new ideas.

Experiment with Different Approaches: Individuals with ADHD may benefit from trying different approaches to creative projects, such as using different mediums or experimenting with different techniques.

Seek Support: It is important for individuals with ADHD to seek support from healthcare professionals, therapists, or support groups. These resources can provide guidance and support in managing ADHD symptoms and harnessing creativity.

While ADHD can pose challenges, research has shown that there may be a link between ADHD and creativity. Individuals with ADHD may have a different way of processing information, leading to unconventional and creative ideas. However, it is important for individuals with ADHD to harness their creativity in a way that is effective and manageable. Strategies such as setting boundaries, breaking projects into smaller tasks, and collaborating with others can help individuals with ADHD stay on task and avoid distraction. Additionally, seeking support from healthcare professionals or support groups can provide guidance and support in managing ADHD symptoms and harnessing creativity. By adopting effective strategies and seeking support, individuals with ADHD can harness their creativity to their advantage and achieve their goals.

The Connection between ADHD and Entrepreneurship

Attention Deficit Hyperactivity Disorder (ADHD) is a neurodevelopmental disorder that can pose challenges in many aspects of life. However, some research suggests that there may be a connection between ADHD and entrepreneurship. In this chapter, we will explore the connection between ADHD and entrepreneurship, as well as some strategies for individuals with ADHD who are interested in starting their own business.

ADHD and Entrepreneurship

ADHD is often associated with challenges such as distractibility, impulsivity, and difficulty with organization and follow-through. However, individuals with ADHD may also possess certain traits that can be advantageous in entrepreneurship. These traits may include:

Creativity: Individuals with ADHD often have a unique way of thinking and may approach problems in unconventional ways, leading to creative ideas and solutions.

Risk-taking: Individuals with ADHD may be more likely to take risks, which can be an important trait in entrepreneurship.

High Energy: Individuals with ADHD often have a high level of energy and may thrive in fast-paced environments, which can be common in entrepreneurship.

Passion: Individuals with ADHD may have a high level of passion for their interests and pursuits, which can be a driving force in entrepreneurship.

While these traits can be advantageous in entrepreneurship, it is important for individuals with ADHD to develop strategies to manage their symptoms and harness their strengths.

Strategies for Individuals with ADHD in Entrepreneurship

Develop a Support System: Starting a business can be overwhelming and stressful, so it is important for individuals with ADHD to have a support system in place. This may include family, friends, or a mentor who can provide guidance and support.

Create a Routine: Individuals with ADHD may struggle with organization and follow-through, so creating a routine can be helpful in staying on track. Setting a schedule for work and taking breaks can help individuals with ADHD stay focused and avoid burnout.

Break Tasks into Smaller, Manageable Steps: Large projects can be overwhelming for individuals with ADHD, so breaking them into smaller, manageable steps can make the process more manageable.

Delegate Tasks: Delegating tasks to others can help individuals with ADHD stay focused on their strengths and avoid burnout. This can also allow individuals with ADHD to focus on tasks they enjoy and are passionate about.

Use Technology: Technology can be a helpful tool for individuals with ADHD. There are many apps and tools available to help with organization, time management, and task tracking.

Focus on Strengths: It is important for individuals with ADHD to focus on their strengths and interests when starting a business. By focusing on tasks, they enjoy and are passionate about, individuals with ADHD can harness their creativity and energy to drive their business forward.

Build a Team: Building a team can be helpful for individuals with ADHD. Having a team in place can provide support and guidance and can also provide different perspectives and ideas.

While ADHD can pose challenges, it can also provide unique strengths that can be advantageous in entrepreneurship. Traits such as creativity, risk-taking, high energy, and passion can be valuable in starting and growing a business. However, it is important for individuals with ADHD to develop strategies to manage their symptoms and harness their strengths. Creating a support system, developing a routine, breaking tasks into smaller steps, and using technology can be helpful in managing ADHD symptoms and staying focused on business goals. By focusing on their strengths and building a team, individuals with ADHD can start and grow successful businesses.

The Connection Between ADHD and Innovation

While ADHD can present challenges in various aspects of life, some research suggests that there may be a connection between ADHD and innovation. In this chapter, we will explore the connection between ADHD and innovation, as well as some strategies for individuals with ADHD who are interested in fostering innovation in their lives and careers.

ADHD and Innovation

Innovation refers to the process of creating new ideas, products, or services that improve upon existing ones or address unmet needs. Individuals with ADHD may possess certain traits that can be advantageous in innovation. These traits may include:

Creativity: Individuals with ADHD often have a unique way of thinking and may approach problems in unconventional ways, leading to creative ideas and solutions.

Hyperfocus: While ADHD can cause distractibility, individuals with ADHD may also experience hyperfocus, a state in which they become fully absorbed in a task or idea. This can lead to a deep level of focus and productivity.

Risk-taking: Individuals with ADHD may be more likely to take risks, which can be an important trait in innovation.

Flexibility: Individuals with ADHD may be more adaptable and able to shift gears quickly, which can be important in innovation.

While these traits can be advantageous in innovation, it is important for individuals with ADHD to develop strategies to manage their symptoms and harness their strengths.

Strategies for Individuals with ADHD in Innovation

Embrace Creativity: Individuals with ADHD should embrace their creativity and explore different ways of approaching problems. This may involve brainstorming sessions, experimenting with new approaches, or collaborating with others.

Set Goals: Setting clear goals can help individuals with ADHD stay focused and avoid getting side-tracked. Breaking larger goals into smaller, more manageable steps can help individuals with ADHD stay on track and make progress towards their goals.

Use Hyperfocus to Your Advantage: Hyperfocus can be a powerful tool for individuals with ADHD. By identifying tasks or projects that capture their attention, individuals with ADHD can use their hyperfocus to be productive and make progress towards their goals.

Take Risks: Taking risks can be a scary prospect, but it can also be a valuable tool for innovation. By embracing their willingness to take risks, individuals with ADHD can push the boundaries and explore new possibilities.

Build a Support Network: Innovation can be a challenging process, so it is important for individuals with ADHD to build a support network. This may include friends, family, or colleagues who can provide feedback, support, and encouragement.

Focus on Your Strengths: It is important for individuals with ADHD to focus on their strengths when exploring new ideas or projects. By focusing on tasks that align with their strengths and interests, individuals with ADHD can harness their creativity and passion to drive innovation forward.

Experiment: Experimenting with new ideas and approaches can be an important tool for innovation. By embracing experimentation, individuals with ADHD can explore new possibilities and learn from their successes and failures.

While ADHD can present challenges, it can also provide unique strengths that can be advantageous in innovation. Traits such as creativity, hyperfocus, risk-taking, and flexibility can be valuable in generating new ideas and pushing boundaries. However, it is important for individuals with ADHD to develop strategies to manage their symptoms and harness their strengths. Setting clear goals, using hyperfocus to your advantage, building a support network, and experimenting with new ideas can be helpful in fostering innovation. By embracing their strengths and exploring new possibilities, individuals with ADHD can drive innovation forward and make a positive impact in the world.

ADHD and Relationships: Navigating Social Interactions

Attention Deficit Hyperactivity Disorder (ADHD) can have a significant impact on an individual's social interactions and relationships. The symptoms of ADHD, such as impulsivity, distractibility, and hyperactivity, can make it challenging for individuals with ADHD to navigate social situations effectively. In this chapter, we will explore the impact of ADHD on relationships and offer strategies for individuals with ADHD to navigate social interactions and foster positive relationships.

Impact of ADHD on Relationships

ADHD can present unique challenges in relationships, such as:

Distractibility: Individuals with ADHD may struggle to maintain focus during conversations, leading them to miss important details or appear disinterested.

Impulsivity: Individuals with ADHD may act impulsively in social situations, such as interrupting others or speaking before thinking, which can lead to misunderstandings or hurt feelings.

Hyperactivity: Individuals with ADHD may struggle to sit still or maintain a quiet demeanour, which can be disruptive in social situations.

Difficulty with Planning and Organization: Individuals with ADHD may struggle with planning and organizing social events or activities, which can make it challenging to maintain social connections.

These challenges can create misunderstandings or conflicts in relationships, which can strain social connections and lead to feelings of frustration or isolation.

Strategies for Navigating Social Interactions with ADHD

Seek Professional Support: Working with a therapist or counsellor can be helpful in developing strategies to manage symptoms of ADHD and improve social skills. A therapist can provide guidance on communication skills, social cues, and emotional regulation, which can be valuable in navigating social interactions.

Practice Active Listening: Individuals with ADHD can improve their listening skills by practicing active listening techniques, such as repeating what the other person has said or asking clarifying questions.

Take Breaks: Individuals with ADHD may need to take breaks during social interactions to manage symptoms of hyperactivity or distractibility. Excusing oneself for a few minutes can be helpful in managing these symptoms and regaining focus.

Develop a Routine: Developing a routine for social events or activities can be helpful in managing symptoms of ADHD. This may involve planning ahead, arriving early, and taking breaks as needed.

Be Mindful of Communication: Individuals with ADHD may benefit from being mindful of their communication style, such as speaking clearly and directly and avoiding interrupting others.

Set Boundaries: Setting clear boundaries can be helpful in managing impulsivity and maintaining healthy relationships. This may involve taking time to think before responding or setting limits on social activities to avoid burnout.

Join Support Groups: Joining support groups or communities for individuals with ADHD can provide a sense of community and support. These groups can offer a safe space to discuss challenges and share strategies for managing symptoms.

The Connection Between ADHD and Substance Abuse

Attention Deficit Hyperactivity Disorder (ADHD) is a neurodevelopmental disorder that affects approximately 5% of children and 2.5% of adults worldwide. Individuals with ADHD often experience difficulties with impulse control, hyperactivity, and attention span. These challenges can lead to additional problems, such as academic and occupational difficulties, relationship challenges, and mental health issues. One common issue that individuals with ADHD may face is substance abuse. In this chapter, we will explore the connection between ADHD and substance abuse, risk factors, and strategies for prevention and treatment.

The Link between ADHD and Substance Abuse

Research has shown that individuals with ADHD are at a higher risk for substance abuse than those without the disorder. A study by the National Institute on Drug Abuse found that individuals with ADHD were twice as likely to develop a substance use disorder as those without ADHD. This increased risk may be due to a combination of genetic, environmental, and psychological factors.

One theory is that individuals with ADHD may turn to substances as a form of self-medication. ADHD can cause feelings of restlessness, impulsivity, and anxiety, and individuals may use substances to cope with these symptoms. Additionally, individuals with ADHD may struggle with boredom or lack of stimulation, and substances may provide a temporary sense of excitement or pleasure.

Risk Factors for Substance Abuse in Individuals with ADHD

While not all individuals with ADHD will develop a substance use disorder, there are several risk factors that increase the likelihood. These include:

Impulsivity: Individuals with ADHD who struggle with impulse control may be more likely to engage in risky behaviours, such as using drugs or alcohol.

Social Isolation: Individuals with ADHD may struggle with social interactions, which can lead to feelings of loneliness or isolation. Substance use may be a way to cope with these feelings or to fit in with peers.

Mental Health Issues: Individuals with ADHD are at a higher risk for co-occurring mental health issues, such as anxiety or depression. These issues can increase the likelihood of substance abuse.

Genetics: There is evidence that genetic factors may contribute to both ADHD and substance use disorders, which may increase the likelihood of co-occurrence.

Prevention and Treatment Strategies

Prevention and treatment strategies for substance abuse in individuals with ADHD should address both the underlying ADHD symptoms and the substance use disorder. Strategies may include:

Medication: Medications used to treat ADHD, such as stimulants, can be effective in reducing symptoms of ADHD and decreasing the likelihood of substance abuse.

Behavioural Therapy: Behavioural therapies, such as Cognitive Behavioural Therapy (CBT), can help individuals with ADHD develop coping skills and strategies for managing symptoms.

Social Support: Social support from friends, family, or support groups can help individuals with ADHD manage symptoms and avoid substance use.

Education: Education on the risks of substance use and the potential consequences can be helpful in preventing substance abuse in individuals with ADHD.

Early Intervention: Early intervention for ADHD and substance use disorders can be critical in preventing long-term consequences and improving outcomes.

The connection between ADHD and substance abuse is complex, and there is no one-size-fits-all solution. However, by understanding the risk factors and implementing prevention and treatment strategies, individuals with ADHD can reduce their likelihood of developing a substance use disorder. Medication, behavioral therapy, social support, education, and early intervention can all play a role in preventing and treating substance abuse in individuals with ADHD. It is important for individuals with ADHD to seek professional support if they are struggling with substance use, as early intervention can improve outcomes and prevent long-term consequences.

The Connection Between ADHD and Sleep Disorders

Attention deficit hyperactivity disorder (ADHD) is a neurodevelopmental disorder that affects both children and adults. It is characterized by symptoms such as inattention, hyperactivity, and impulsivity, which can cause difficulties in various areas of life. One area that is often affected by ADHD is sleep. Many individuals with ADHD have difficulty falling asleep, staying asleep, and waking up. In this chapter, we will explore the connection between ADHD and sleep disorders.

Sleep disorders in individuals with ADHD

Individuals with ADHD are more likely to have sleep problems than those without the disorder. One study found that up to 75% of children with ADHD experience sleep problems, compared to approximately 20% of children without ADHD. The most common sleep problems in individuals with ADHD are:

Difficulty falling asleep: Individuals with ADHD may have difficulty falling asleep because their minds are often racing with thoughts and ideas.

Difficulty staying asleep: Once individuals with ADHD are asleep, they may have trouble staying asleep due to their hyperactivity, restlessness, or anxiety.

Sleep apnea: Some individuals with ADHD may also have sleep apnea, which is a condition in which breathing stops and starts during sleep.

Circadian rhythm disorder: Individuals with ADHD may also experience circadian rhythm disorder, which means their body clock is not synchronized with their sleep-wake cycle.

Delayed sleep phase syndrome: This is a condition in which an individual's sleep-wake cycle is delayed by a few hours, making it difficult for them to fall asleep and wake up at typical times.

The impact of sleep disorders on individuals with ADHD

The sleep disorders experienced by individuals with ADHD can have a significant impact on their daily lives. Sleep deprivation can exacerbate ADHD symptoms such as inattention, impulsivity, and hyperactivity, making it more difficult to manage these symptoms. In addition, lack of sleep can lead to irritability, mood swings, and difficulty regulating emotions.

Poor sleep can also affect academic and occupational performance. Children with ADHD who do not get enough sleep may struggle in school and have difficulty concentrating. Adults with ADHD who experience sleep problems may have difficulty staying focused at work or completing tasks on time.

Furthermore, sleep disorders in individuals with ADHD can also increase the risk of other health problems. Sleep apnea, for example, is associated with an increased risk of heart disease, stroke, and diabetes.

Treatment options for sleep disorders in individuals with ADHD

There are various treatment options available for individuals with ADHD who experience sleep disorders. One of the most common treatments is medication. Stimulant medications used to treat ADHD, such as Ritalin and Adderall, can also help individuals with ADHD fall asleep and stay asleep. However, these medications can also interfere with sleep, so it is important to take them at the appropriate time.

Non-pharmacological treatments for sleep disorders in individuals with ADHD include cognitive-behavioral therapy (CBT). CBT is a type of talk therapy that helps individuals identify and change negative thoughts and behaviours that may be contributing to their sleep problems. CBT can also help individuals establish a regular sleep routine, which can improve their sleep quality.

Other non-pharmacological treatments for sleep disorders in individuals with ADHD include relaxation techniques such as meditation, yoga, and deep breathing exercises. These techniques can help individuals with ADHD calm their minds and bodies, making it easier to fall asleep.

The Connection Between ADHD and Anxiety Disorders

Attention Deficit Hyperactivity Disorder (ADHD) is a neurodevelopmental disorder characterized by symptoms of inattention, hyperactivity, and impulsivity. Although these symptoms are commonly associated with ADHD, the disorder can manifest itself in many different ways. One of the most common co-occurring conditions in individuals with ADHD is anxiety disorders. In this chapter, we will explore the connection between ADHD and anxiety disorders.

Anxiety disorders are a group of mental disorders characterized by excessive fear or worry about everyday situations. These disorders can significantly impair an individual's daily functioning and quality of life. Anxiety disorders can include generalized anxiety disorder, panic disorder, social anxiety disorder, and specific phobias.

Studies have shown that individuals with ADHD are at a higher risk of developing anxiety disorders than those without ADHD. In fact, up to 50% of individuals with ADHD will also experience anxiety disorders at some point in their lives.

So, what is the connection between ADHD and anxiety disorders? The answer lies in the brain. Both ADHD and anxiety disorders have been linked to imbalances in neurotransmitters such as serotonin, norepinephrine, and dopamine. Individuals with ADHD have lower levels of these neurotransmitters in the prefrontal cortex, which is responsible for regulating attention and impulse control.

The prefrontal cortex is also connected to the amygdala, which is the part of the brain that controls fear and anxiety. Studies have shown that the amygdala is overactive in individuals with anxiety disorders, leading to increased fear and worry. This overactivity can also affect the prefrontal cortex, leading to difficulties with attention and impulse control.

Additionally, the symptoms of ADHD can also contribute to the development of anxiety disorders. Individuals with ADHD often experience difficulties with social interactions, organization, and time management, which can lead to feelings of stress and anxiety.

Furthermore, individuals with ADHD may also experience rejection sensitivity, a phenomenon where they are more sensitive to criticism and rejection than those without ADHD. This sensitivity can lead to anxiety in social situations, as individuals with ADHD may fear rejection or negative feedback.

It is important to note that anxiety disorders can also develop independently of ADHD. However, the high comorbidity rate between these two disorders highlights the importance of screening individuals with ADHD for anxiety disorders and vice versa.

So, what can be done to manage the co-occurrence of ADHD and anxiety disorders? Treatment options for both disorders may include medication, psychotherapy, or a combination of both. Stimulant medications commonly used to treat ADHD have also been found to be effective in treating anxiety disorders.

Cognitive-behavioral therapy (CBT) is a type of psychotherapy that has been found to be effective in treating both ADHD and anxiety disorders. CBT focuses on identifying and changing negative thought patterns and behaviours, which can lead to a reduction in anxiety symptoms.

Additionally, lifestyle changes such as exercise, relaxation techniques, and improving sleep habits can also be beneficial for managing symptoms of both ADHD and anxiety disorders.

The Connection Between ADHD and Depression

Attention Deficit Hyperactivity Disorder (ADHD) is a neurodevelopmental disorder that affects approximately 5% of children and 2.5% of adults in the United Kingdom. ADHD is often characterized by symptoms such as impulsivity, hyperactivity, and inattention. While these symptoms can make everyday life challenging, individuals with ADHD are also at a higher risk of developing comorbid conditions such as anxiety and depression.

Depression is a mood disorder that can cause feelings of sadness, hopelessness, and a lack of interest in activities that were previously enjoyable. Depression can also cause physical symptoms such as fatigue, changes in appetite, and sleep disturbances. ADHD and depression often co-occur, and researchers have been trying to understand the link between the two conditions.

Studies have shown that individuals with ADHD are at a higher risk of developing depression compared to those without ADHD. A meta-analysis of 23 studies found that the risk of developing depression was two to three times higher in individuals with ADHD than in those without ADHD. The onset of depression in individuals with ADHD typically occurs during adolescence or early adulthood.

There are several reasons why individuals with ADHD may be at a higher risk of developing depression. One reason is that the symptoms of ADHD, such as inattention and impulsivity, can lead to difficulties in school or work, social interactions, and relationships. These difficulties can lead to feelings of frustration, low self-esteem, and hopelessness, which are also common symptoms of depression.

Another reason why ADHD and depression are often comorbid is that they may share similar underlying neurobiological mechanisms. Research has suggested that ADHD and depression may be related to dysfunction in the prefrontal cortex of the brain, which is responsible for regulating attention, impulse control, and emotion regulation. Dysfunction in this area of the brain may contribute to both ADHD symptoms and depression symptoms.

Treating depression in individuals with ADHD can be challenging. While medication such as antidepressants can be effective in treating depression, they may also worsen ADHD symptoms. Some antidepressants can cause agitation, insomnia, and increased impulsivity, which can exacerbate ADHD symptoms. It is essential to work closely with a healthcare professional to find the right medication and dosage for individuals with ADHD and depression.

Psychotherapy is another treatment option for individuals with ADHD and depression. Cognitive Behavioural Therapy (CBT) has been shown to be effective in treating both conditions. CBT helps individuals with ADHD and depression identify negative thought patterns and develop coping strategies to manage their symptoms. Mindfulness-based therapies such as Mindfulness-Based Cognitive Therapy (MBCT) and Mindfulness-Based Stress Reduction (MBSR) have also shown promise in treating comorbid ADHD and depression.

It is also important to address lifestyle factors that can contribute to both ADHD and depression. Regular exercise, healthy eating habits, and adequate sleep can all help manage symptoms of both conditions. It is also essential to seek support from family, friends, and mental health professionals.

ADHD and Employment: Challenges and Strategies

ADHD is often associated with difficulties in academic settings and social interactions, but it can also impact one's ability to succeed in the workplace. In fact, studies have found that adults with ADHD are more likely to experience job instability, underemployment, and lower incomes than those without the condition. However, with proper support and strategies, individuals with ADHD can thrive in the workplace. This chapter will explore the challenges that individuals with ADHD may face in employment, as well as strategies that can help them succeed.

One of the biggest challenges for individuals with ADHD in the workplace is difficulty with executive functioning skills, such as planning, organizing, prioritizing, and completing tasks. They may also struggle with time management, meeting deadlines, and staying focused on one task at a time. This can lead to issues with productivity, performance, and overall job satisfaction.

In addition, individuals with ADHD may also struggle with social interactions in the workplace. They may have difficulty with communication, listening, and following directions. This can lead to misunderstandings, conflicts with co-workers or supervisors, and ultimately impact their job performance.

However, there are a number of strategies that individuals with ADHD can use to improve their success in the workplace. One important strategy is to create a structured routine and set clear goals and priorities for each day. This can help individuals with ADHD to stay on track and prioritize their tasks in a way that is manageable.

Another important strategy is to break down larger projects into smaller, more manageable tasks. This can help to reduce feelings of overwhelm and allow individuals with ADHD to focus on one task at a time. Additionally, setting specific deadlines for each task can help to improve time management and ensure that projects are completed on time.

It is also important for individuals with ADHD to develop strategies for managing distractions in the workplace. This may include using noise-cancelling headphones, taking breaks to stretch or walk, or using a timer to stay focused on a specific task for a set period of time.

Effective communication is also critical for success in the workplace. Individuals with ADHD may benefit from being upfront with their co-workers or supervisor about their condition and how it impacts their work. This can help to reduce misunderstandings and ensure that everyone is on the same page.

In addition, seeking support from a mental health professional or ADHD coach can be incredibly beneficial for individuals with ADHD. They can provide guidance and support for developing strategies and coping mechanisms for managing symptoms in the workplace.

Finally, it is important for employers to recognize and accommodate the needs of individuals with ADHD in the workplace. This may include providing additional support and resources, such as flexible work schedules, additional training, or access to accommodations such as noise-cancelling headphones or standing desks.

ADHD and Parenting: Navigating the Challenges

Parenting is a challenging task, but it becomes even more challenging when you have a child with ADHD. Attention-deficit/hyperactivity disorder (ADHD) is a neurodevelopmental disorder that affects an estimated 5-10% of children worldwide. Children with ADHD often have difficulties with attention, impulsivity, and hyperactivity, which can make parenting more challenging. However, with the right strategies and support, parents of children with ADHD can help their child thrive.

Understanding ADHD

Before we dive into strategies for parenting a child with ADHD, it's important to understand the disorder. ADHD is a complex condition that affects the brain's executive functions, such as attention, working memory, and self-control. Children with ADHD often struggle with tasks that require sustained attention, organization, and planning. They may also act impulsively and struggle with emotional regulation.

ADHD is not caused by poor parenting or a lack of discipline. It is a neurological condition that has a genetic component. However, environmental factors such as exposure to toxins or prenatal alcohol or tobacco exposure may also play a role in the development of ADHD.

Challenges of Parenting a Child with ADHD

Parenting a child with ADHD can be challenging in many ways. Some of the common challenges parents may face include:

Difficulty with organization: Children with ADHD may struggle with organizing their belongings, homework, and schedule.

Difficulty with time management: Children with ADHD may struggle with estimating time and managing their time effectively.

Difficulty with social skills: Children with ADHD may struggle with making and keeping friends due to their impulsivity and hyperactivity.

Difficulty with emotional regulation: Children with ADHD may struggle with managing their emotions and may become easily frustrated, angry, or overwhelmed.

Difficulty with completing tasks: Children with ADHD may struggle with completing tasks due to their distractibility and difficulty with sustaining attention.

Strategies for Parenting a Child with ADHD

Parenting a child with ADHD can be challenging, but there are several strategies that parents can use to help their child thrive. Here are some effective strategies:

Develop a routine: Children with ADHD benefit from structure and routine. Develop a consistent routine for your child that includes regular mealtimes, homework time, and bedtime.

Use visual aids: Visual aids such as charts and schedules can help children with ADHD stay organized and on track.

Set clear expectations: Children with ADHD benefit from clear and consistent expectations. Be clear about what you expect from your child and establish consequences for not meeting expectations.

Use positive reinforcement: Positive reinforcement such as praise, rewards, and privileges can be effective in encouraging positive behavior in children with ADHD.

Teach coping skills: Children with ADHD may struggle with emotional regulation. Teach your child coping skills such as deep breathing, visualization, and mindfulness to help them manage their emotions.

Encourage physical activity: Children with ADHD benefit from regular physical activity. Encourage your child to participate in sports or other activities that require physical exertion.

Seek professional help: If your child's ADHD is significantly affecting their daily life, seek professional help. A mental health professional can help your child develop coping skills and provide therapy to address emotional and behavioral issues.

ADHD and Advocacy: Empowering Neurodiverse Individuals

ADHD (Attention Deficit Hyperactivity Disorder) affects millions of people worldwide, and yet, there is still a lack of understanding and awareness about this condition. For many people with ADHD, it can be a daily challenge to navigate a world that is not always accommodating to neurodiversity. However, with advocacy and empowerment, people with ADHD can thrive and contribute to society in meaningful ways.

Advocacy is crucial in helping individuals with ADHD gain access to the resources and accommodations they need to succeed. This can include accommodations in the workplace, educational settings, and in the healthcare system. Advocacy can also help to combat the stigma and misconceptions surrounding ADHD, which can lead to discrimination and social exclusion.

One of the most important ways to empower individuals with ADHD is to provide them with education and information about their condition. This includes information about the symptoms, diagnosis, and treatment options available. Many people with ADHD are not diagnosed until later in life, which can lead to feelings of frustration and self-doubt. By providing information and education, individuals with ADHD can better understand their condition and develop strategies to manage their symptoms.

Another crucial aspect of advocacy is ensuring that individuals with ADHD have access to appropriate healthcare services. This includes access to mental health services, which can be an essential component of managing ADHD. Mental health professionals can provide therapy and medication management to help individuals with ADHD manage their symptoms effectively.

It is also essential to ensure that individuals with ADHD have access to educational opportunities that cater to their unique learning styles. Many individuals with ADHD struggle in traditional educational settings, which can lead to academic underachievement and low self-esteem. By providing accommodations and support, such as extra time on exams, preferential seating, and assistive technology, individuals with ADHD can thrive academically.

In the workplace, individuals with ADHD may face unique challenges due to their symptoms. These can include difficulties with time management, distractibility, and forgetfulness. However, with appropriate accommodations and support, individuals with ADHD can be highly productive and successful in their careers. This may include accommodations such as flexible schedules, clear instructions, and a structured work environment.

Parents of children with ADHD may also face unique challenges. Raising a child with ADHD can be challenging, as their symptoms can impact their behavior, academic performance, and social interactions. However, with the right support and resources, parents can help their children with ADHD succeed. This may include working with their child's school to provide accommodations and support, finding mental health services, and connecting with other parents of children with ADHD for support and advice.

Empowering individuals with ADHD also involves advocating for policies and laws that promote neurodiversity and inclusion. This can include advocating for workplace accommodations, educational support, and access to mental health services. It can also include advocating for changes in societal attitudes towards ADHD and other neurodiverse conditions. By advocating for neurodiversity and inclusion, we can create a world where individuals with ADHD are valued and respected for their unique strengths and talents.

END

Thank you for taking the time to read this Introduction to a Neurodiverse World book.
We have a range of books within this series that are steadily being released.
Topics Cover

- Autism
- ADHD
- Sensory Processing Disorder (SPD)
- Pathological Demand Avoidance (PDA)
- Avoidant Restrictive Food Intake Disorder (ARFID)

We also post weekly Articles on our website and our social media sites (links Below)

Divergent Consultants Ltd are accredited Counsellors and Psychotherapists who specialise in Spectrum Disorders.

Started by Gareth Croot when his 3-year-old Non-Verbal son was diagnosed with Autism Spectrum Disorder, Global Development Delay and Hypermobility.
This lead his family on a journey resulting in his 12 year old daughter starting the ASD diagnostic pathway and Gareth also being diagnosed with Autism, PDA, Hypermobility and currently awaiting ADHD assessment.
Divergent Consultants offer introduction to Autism Courses, Sleep Therapy Courses, Pre and Post diagnosis counselling for parents and newly diagnosed adults aswell as general support functions
you can visit us at www.divergentconsultants.co.uk
Facebook https://www.facebook.com/people/Divergent-Consultants/100088643106730/
TikTok https://www.tiktok.com/divergentconsultants
Instagram
https://www.instagram.com/divergent_consultants/

Printed in Great Britain
by Amazon